GETTING STARTED WITH ZOOM

A BEGINNERS GUIDE TO VIDEOCONFERENCING

SCOTT LA COUNTE

RIDICULOUSLY
SIMPLE BOOKS

ANAHEIM, CALIFORNIA

www.RidiculouslySimpleBooks.com

Table of Contents

Disclaimer: *Please note, while every effort has been made to ensure accuracy, this book is not endorsed by Zoom Video Communications, Inc. and should be considered unofficial.*

INTRODUCTION

Times have certainly changed.

It wasn't that long ago when videoconferencing was cutting edge. It was something expensive companies did for board meetings with people who couldn't make it in.

This is still true today, but videoconferencing has evolved. Today it's used both globally and regionally to connect remote workers.

As more and more companies are switching to either partially remote or fully remote workplace environments, understanding videoconferencing is a must.

Like most software today, Zoom is pretty easy to get up and running, but it takes time to learn its most powerful features. This book will walk you through what you need to know to become a Zoom power user.

[1]
WELCOME TO ZOOM

This chapter will cover:
- Zoom's pricing model
- What makes Zoom unique
- How to sign up

UNDERSTANDING ZOOM PRICING

The first question most people are going to have when they sign up for Zoom is probably a financial one: should I pay? Zoom's free plan is a full-feature product. In fact, almost all of this book will cover features that you don't have to pay for!

So, why on Earth would you pay for something that's free?

The answer to that largely depends on how you will be using it, so this section will cover which plan is right for you.

The biggest caveat of the free plan centers around the meeting duration limit: it's 40-minutes (unless you have less than three people).

The free plan is limited to one host and 100 users. That's probably plenty for most people. If you need more, then that's where an upgrade will help. Enterprise plans can have up to 1,000 participants on a call.

The next level up from free is the Basic plan ($14.99 per month per host). This lets you host meetings for up to 24-hours—but seriously, if you're hosting a 24-hour meeting, then maybe it's time you take a vacation because that's intense! You also get a personal meeting ID which comes in handy if you have the same meeting every week. This way you can give people a link for where the meeting is happening instead of having to give everyone a link more last minute each time it happens. Finally, you can record a meeting to the cloud (on the free plan, you can record a meeting locally—i.e. on your computer's hard drive).

For most small businesses, the Basic plan will work out great. There are two big features that might make upgrading to the Pro plan ($19.99 per month per host) beneficial: one, the pro plan bumps you up to 300 participants; and two, you can have your own company branding—that may be useful if you have a lot of clients and you want your meeting to have a more high-end feel.

It should also be noted that Zoom also offers plans specific to different industries like Education and Telehealth.

Finally, it should be noted that there are premium Zoom add-ons. The biggest one is for webinars. You could technically host one through your free or paid account, but there is a $40 per month webinar plan that offers features like Q&A and the ability to show the webinar live to Facebook or YouTube.

ZOOM VS. GOOGLE MEET (FORMERLY HANGOUTS)

The next question a lot of users will probably have is why Zoom? There are other videoconferencing companies out there. Zoom is perhaps the best known, but what about Google Meet? That's free and integrates perfectly into your Google Account.

It really comes down to you and your business. Google Meet is amazing software. It's great for smaller meetups—and can even handle larger ones.

The biggest difference between the two comes down to features. Google Meet is very basic. It's stripped of almost all the features that will be covered in this book. That might work out well for short daily scrum calls, but hosting a larger meeting that needs breakaway meetings will be more problematic.

There are also smaller details—like Google Meet doesn't let you have a custom background, which has become the favorite feature of many Zoom users.

SIGNING UP

Signing up to Zoom is pretty straightforward. Go to Zoom.us and click the signup button.

SIGN UP, IT'S FREE

The first thing you'll see is an age verification form. I know some people like to lie about their age, I don't recommend it here—especially since this is all private—but if you do it, make sure you do it in a way that you are over 18.

For verification, please confirm your date of birth.

| Month | ⌄ | Day | ⌄ | Year | ⌄ | Continue |

This data will not be stored

If you add an age younger than 18, then you'll be greeted with a message about not being eligible to sign up for Zoom.

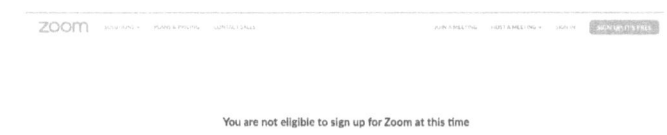

You are not eligible to sign up for Zoom at this time

That message won't go away if you refresh your browser; the only way to clear it so you can sign up is to clear your cache or use another browser.

Once you add your age, you'll need to either add your work email (i.e. the email clients and colleagues contact you) or sign in with SSO (for users that are logging in to a company's custom Zoom domain—most users will not use this), Google, or Facebook.

I recommend Google. There are no passwords to remember. But it's really up to you. Using one or the other doesn't give you any account benefits within Zoom.

Sign Up Free

Your work email address

Zoom is protected by reCAPTCHA and the Privacy Policy and Terms of Service apply.

Sign Up

Already have an account? Sign in.

or

🔍   Sign in with SSO

G   Sign in with Google

f   Sign in with Facebook

If you choose Sign in with Google, then it will ask you what Google account you want to use.

G   Sign in with Google

Choose an account

to continue to Zoom

Once you're signed up, you'll see your account dashboard.

Free and paid accounts will have a similar look and feel. I'll be using a free account for the first part of this book, and then switching to a paid account to cover some of the admin features (like user and room management).

If you decide to upgrade at any time, there's an option on the top that says Plans & Pricing that outlines all the various plans.

[2]
GETTING STARTED

This chapter will cover:
- Editing your profile
- Setting up a meeting
- Meeting options
- Meeting templates
- Settings

EDITING YOUR PROFILE

Once you sign up for Zoom, you are technically ready to go—you can start your first meeting right away.

I recommend holding off on that and updating your profile first. You can do that by clicking on Profile to your left.

Anything that can be changed has a blue Edit option next to it (or change for profile picture). The reason I recommend going here is twofold: one, if you used your personal email account, it may have an avatar that you don't want work people to see, or it may have a nickname instead of your real name (for example, mine says "Scott Douglas," which is my pen name for many books); two, you may need to update the time zone—this will make sure you don't miss meetings (if you get a sched-uled meeting and you have the wrong time zone listed, then you'll get the wrong time and will miss the meeting).

When you click the Edit next to your name, you'll also be given the option to add things like your phone number, job title, and your location. It's all optional but may be beneficial depending on how you are using the account.

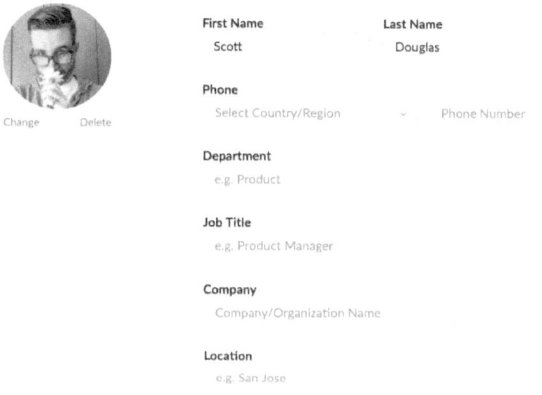

Near the bottom of the profile page is a place to sync your calendar; that way if you get invited to a meeting, then you'll see it in your Google Calendar (or whatever meeting you have synced).

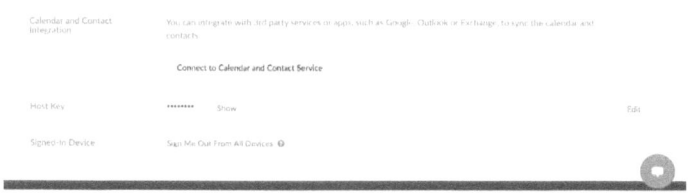

If you change anything here, make sure you save it.

HOSTING YOUR FIRST MEETING

Before you can start a meeting, you have to schedule a meeting. Don't worry: if you want to start it right away, there's going to be a way to do it. But you still have to start with scheduling it.

To get started, go to Meetings on your right, and click the blue Schedule a New Meeting.

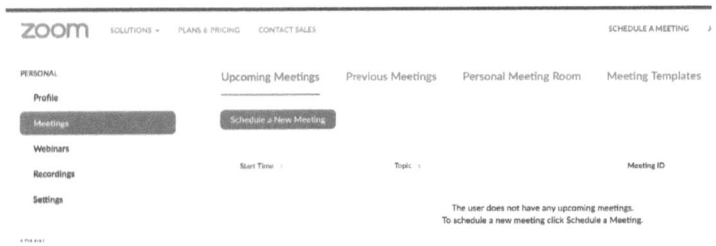

Next, add in your meeting details. Technically, you don't have to do anything here. You can just accept all the defaults. But adding details will help make the meeting more identifiable. For example, having a unique name like "Morning Standup Call" is going to help when you have several meetings scheduled. If you are on the free plan, you'll also see the warning about 40-minute calls.

My Meetings   Schedule a Meeting

Schedule a Meeting

Topic	My Meeting
Description (Optional)	Enter your meeting description
When	07/06/2020 1:00 ⌄ PM ⌄
Duration	1 ⌄ hr 0 ⌄ min

Your Zoom Basic plan has a 40-minute time limit on meetings with 3 or more participants. Upgrade now to enjoy unlimited group meetings. Upgrade Now

Do not show this message again

Time Zone	(GMT-7:00) Pacific Time (US and Canada) ⌄
	Recurring meeting
Meeting ID	Personal Meeting ID
	⊙ Generate Automatically

Near the bottom, there are two things of particular note. One is the option that says Video. This does not mean that this will not be a video call. It just means the video is turned off when people first join. This is recommended so people have time to adjust themself before people see their face. The second thing you should pay attention to is the Meeting Options. If you want people to be able to join in before you get there, for example, you can check off the first option to Enable join before host. You can also mute everyone as they arrive. Finally, you can Record the meeting automatically on your computer (if you don't check this off, then there's an option to record once the meeting has begun). Once you have everything saved, select Save.

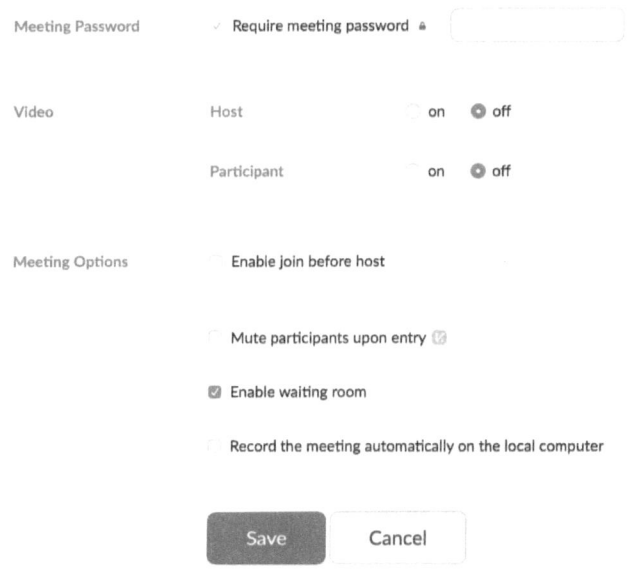

After you save your meeting, you'll see it as an upcoming meeting. From here you have the option to delete it or to start it. So if you want to start it ASAP, then just click Start.

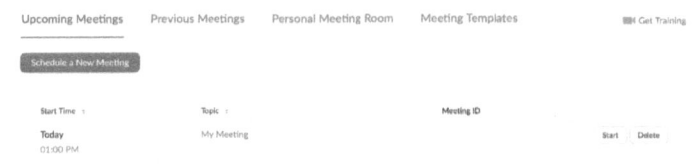

MEETING OPTIONS

Before looking at what happens when you start a meeting, let's look briefly at the three other meeting tabs in the Meeting menu.

If you see something in this book that isn't in your version of Zoom, the reason is very likely the setting is toggled off. Toggle it on, and restart the software, then you should see it.

PREVIOUS MEETING

As the name implies, the first option shows all of your previous meetings. You can delete any of these, or you can start them again.

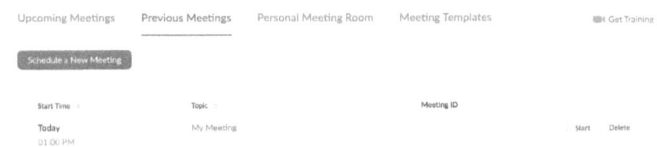

PERSONAL MEETING ROOM

I said that you need to schedule a meeting before starting a meeting. This is technically true, but there is an option to start what's called a personal meeting. This is more of a private one-on-one meeting. It's sort of what you would do more on the fly—an unscheduled meeting to go over something briefly.

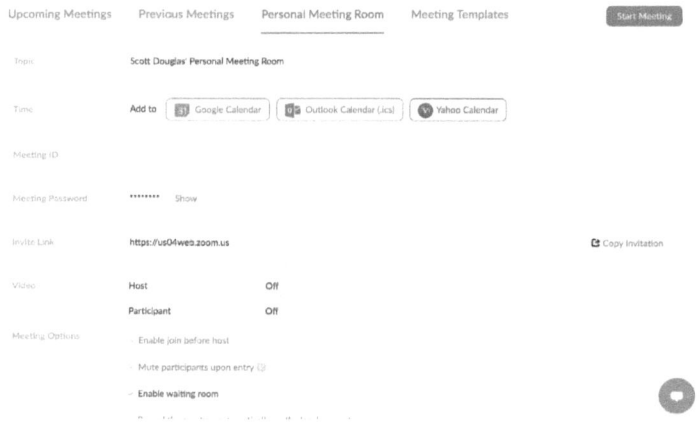

MEETING TEMPLATES

Meeting templates help you save time by saving common meetings. Let's say you have a lot of ten-minute scrum meetings. You can save one meeting as a template and then just copy that template anytime you want to start a similar meeting.

By default, the tab is obviously blank because you haven't saved any.

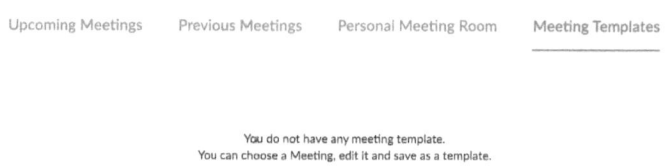

If you go into your upcoming meetings or previous meeting then click the name of any meeting, you can open up the meeting details. Scroll to the very bottom and you'll see an option to save the meeting as a template.

Save as a Meeting Template

If you return to Meeting Templates, then you'll now see an option to schedule the meeting with the template. You can save up to 40 templates.

Upcoming Meetings	Previous Meetings	Personal Meeting Room	Meeting Templates	Get

You have saved 1 template(s) so far. You can save up to 40 templates

Template Name	Modify Time	Action	
My Meeting	Jul 6, 2020 03:00 PM	Schedule Meeting with this Template	Delete

SETTINGS

The last section under the Personal menu is for settings.

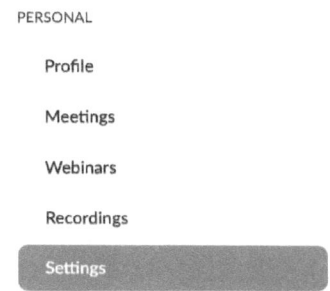

PERSONAL

Profile

Meetings

Webinars

Recordings

Settings

When you access this area, you'll see a tab menu across the top with three options: Meeting, Recording, and Telephone.

Meeting   Recording   Telephone

I'm going to go a little backwards in this second because most of the things we are covering are in the first area. Very briefly, however, let's look at the other two menus: Recording and Telephone.

Recording is where you can go to change by whom and how an online conference can be recorded. You can also toggle on and off if you want it to record automatically and if you want a disclaimer so anyone joining in knows they are being recorded.

Meeting   Recording   Telephone

Recording

Local recording
Allow hosts and participants to record the meeting to a local file

☑ Hosts can give participants the permission to record locally

Automatic recording
Record meetings automatically as they start

Recording disclaimer
Show a customizable disclaimer to participants before a recording starts ☑

Multiple audio notifications of recorded meeting
Play notification messages to participants who join the meeting audio. These messages play each time the recording starts or restarts, informing participants that the meeting is being recorded. If participants join the audio from telephone, even if this option is disabled, users will hear one notification message per meeting.

The last menu, Telephone, contains just two options that are both just on / off toggles. One is to show international numbers on the invitation email and the other is to hide phone numbers of people calling in.

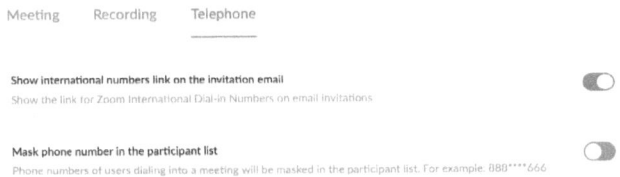

SETTINGS (BASIC)

Most of the meeting settings are just toggles and they're self-explanatory. There are a few worth pointing out in a little more detail, however. The first are under the Basic Settings menu.

The Chat feature is something you should pay particular attention to. Depending on the users, you might want to have it off entirely. I'll go more into how chatting works on Zoom later in this book, but for now, just know there are options here to limit it.

Anything with a V next to it means it's only on certain versions of Zoom—usually 4.0 or later: at this writing, version 5.1.0.

In Meeting (Basic)

Require encryption for 3rd party endpoints (SIP/H.323)

By default, Zoom requires encryption for all data transferred between the Zoom cloud, Zoom client, and Zoom Room. Turn on this setting to require encryption for 3rd party endpoints (SIP/H.323) as well.

Chat

Allow meeting participants to send a message visible to all participants

Prevent participants from saving chat ☑

Private chat

Allow meeting participants to send a private 1:1 message to another participant.

Auto saving chats

Automatically save all in-meeting chats so that hosts do not need to manually save the text of the chat after the meeting starts.

Sound notification when someone joins or leaves

Under File Transfers, there is an option to limit what can be sent; if, for example, you only want Word files shared—not photos or videos—you can save it there. To allow only certain files, check off the Only allow specific file types.

Show Zoom windows during share screen is more of a preference; by default when you are sharing your screen doing a presentation, you can't see anyone else; toggling this on shows you participants.

File transfer

Hosts and participants can send files through the in-meeting chat.
☑

   ☐ Only allow specified file types ☑

Feedback to Zoom

Add a Feedback tab to the Windows Settings or Mac Preferences
dialog, and also enable users to provide feedback to Zoom at the end
of the meeting

Display end-of-meeting experience feedback survey

Display a thumbs up/down survey at the end of each meeting. If
participants respond with thumbs down, they can provide additional
information about what went wrong. ☑

Always show meeting control toolbar

Always show meeting controls during a meeting ☑

Show Zoom windows during screen share ☑

Screen sharing

Allow host and participants to share their screen or content during
meetings

I'll cover annotations and whiteboards later, but
be aware that by default people can save these; if
you don't want them to, uncheck the box.

Who can share?

○ Host Only   All Participants ⑦

Who can start sharing when someone else is sharing?

○ Host Only   All Participants ⑦

Disable desktop/screen share for users

Disable desktop or screen share in a meeting and only allow sharing of selected applications. ⑦

Annotation

Allow host and participants to use annotation tools to add information to shared screens ⑦

☑ Allow saving of shared screens with annotations ⑦

○ By default, only the user who is sharing can annotate ⑦

Whiteboard

Allow host and participants to share whiteboard during a meeting ⑦

☑ Allow saving of whiteboard content ⑦

○ Auto save whiteboard content when sharing is stopped

If you are doing any kind of survey in your conference, then Nonverbal feedback is an option you might want toggled on; it lets users nonverbally give feedback by clicking on buttons.

Remote control

During screen sharing, the person who is sharing can allow others to control the shared content

Nonverbal feedback

Participants in a meeting can provide nonverbal feedback and express opinions by clicking on icons in the Participants panel. ⓥ

Allow removed participants to rejoin

Allows previously removed meeting participants and webinar panelists to rejoin ⓥ

Allow participants to rename themselves

Allow meeting participants and webinar panelists to rename themselves. ⓥ

Hide participant profile pictures in a meeting

All participant profile pictures will be hidden and only the names of participants will be displayed on the video screen. Participants will not be able to update their profile pictures in the meeting. ⓥ

SETTINGS (ADVANCED)

I'll cover Breakout Rooms later in this book; these special rooms give you the ability to have mini sessions within your conference. For example, 100 people join your meeting; 30 minutes into it, you can have a breakout session of 10 groups of 10; they go off and have mini sessions, then return to the main room after. To use them, make sure you toggle this on (it's off by default).

Closed captioning is also an option here. If you want people to read what the person is saying, then toggle it on here; keep in mind, however, someone has to manually type the captions.

Report participants to Zoom

Hosts can report meeting participants for inappropriate behavior to Zoom's Trust and Safety team for review. This setting can be found on the Security icon on the meeting controls toolbar. ⊽

Breakout room

Allow host to split meeting participants into separate, smaller rooms

Remote support

Allow meeting host to provide 1:1 remote support to another participant

Closed captioning

Allow host to type closed captions or assign a participant/third party device to add closed captions

Save Captions

Allow participants to save fully closed captions or transcripts

Far end camera control

Allow another user to take control of your camera during a meeting. Both users (the one requesting control and the one giving control) must have this option turned on.

Most people love virtual backgrounds—or at least don't get upset when other people have them. Some people find them unprofessional and annoying. If you are of the latter, you can disable anyone from using them here.

Virtual background

Customize your background to keep your environment private from others in a meeting. This can be used with or without a green screen.

☑ Allow use of videos for virtual backgrounds ⒱

Identify guest participants in the meeting/webinar

Participants who belong to your account can see that a guest (someone who does not belong to your account) is participating in the meeting/webinar. The Participants list indicates which attendees are guests. The guests themselves do not see that they are listed as guests. ⒱

Auto-answer group in chat

Enable users to see and add contacts to 'auto-answer group' in the contact list on chat. Any call from members of this group will be automatically answered.

Only show default email when sending email invites

Allow users to invite participants by email only by using the default email program selected on their computer

Use HTML format email for Outlook plugin

Use HTML formatting instead of plain text for meeting invitations scheduled with the Outlook plugin

I mentioned earlier that you need to install Zoom software to use it; that's not entirely true. The host can actually enable users to use their browser by toggling this on. It's off by default because many features are not available in the web browser based version of Zoom.

Allow users to select stereo audio in their client settings

Allow users to select stereo audio during a meeting

Allow users to select original sound in their client settings

Allow users to select original sound during a meeting

Show a "Join from your browser" link

Allow participants to bypass the Zoom application download process, and join a meeting directly from their browser. This is a workaround for participants who are unable to download, install, or run applications. Note that the meeting experience from the browser is limited

SETTINGS (OTHER)

If you want other people to schedule meetings on your behalf, you can assign a person by adding their information in the Assign scheduling privilege to section.

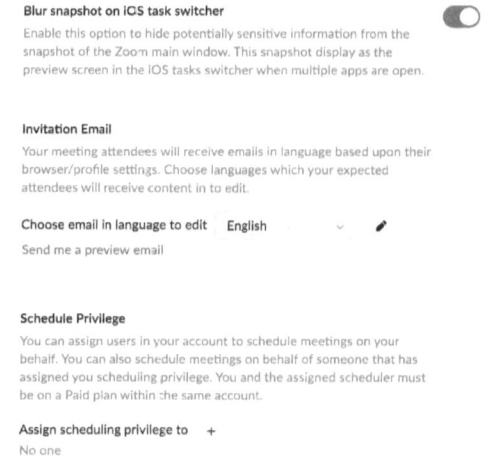

[3]

YOUR FIRST VIDEOCALL

This chapter will cover:
- Starting a meeting
- Basic meeting features
- Virtual background
- Chatting in Zoom
- Breakout sessions
- Changing window views

STARTING A MEETING

To start any meeting, find the meeting and click the Start Meeting button. But what about the people that are attending it? You have two options:

One, open the meeting by clicking on the name, and then scrolling down until you see the invite link.

From here, click the Copy Invitation option. This brings up a box with the meeting information. Click the copy button again, and then go into your email and create an email to the people who are going and paste this message inside of it.

The second option requires you to download a small add-on for either Outlook or Chrome. This lets you schedule meetings right in your Outlook or Google Calendar.

Save time by scheduling your meetings directly from your calendar.

 Microsoft Outlook Plugin
Add Zoom

 Chrome Extension
Download

ZOOM CONFERENCE BASICS

Now that the person has their invite, let's start a meeting and see how to use it.

The first thing you will see is a box asking you to open Zoom. Zoom requires software on your computer—it is not cloud-based. Assuming you have it, then click the open button; if you don't, then click the Download option on the webpage.

zoom

Open zoom.us?

When system dialog prompts, click **Open zoom.us**.

If you have Zoom Client installed, launch meeting. Otherwise, download and run Zoom.

The next thing you'll see is the Zoom software with a message asking you to join with Computer

Audio. You can click the option below that if you want to test your audio first.

At this point, you have the option to invite people to the conference. Or you can wait for them to show up.

Invite Others

When someone comes, you'll see a message with their name and the option to remove or admit them. You can also click Message to send them a note—such as the meeting will start in five more minutes; until you click Admit, they are in a virtual waiting room and cannot see what's going on in the conference.

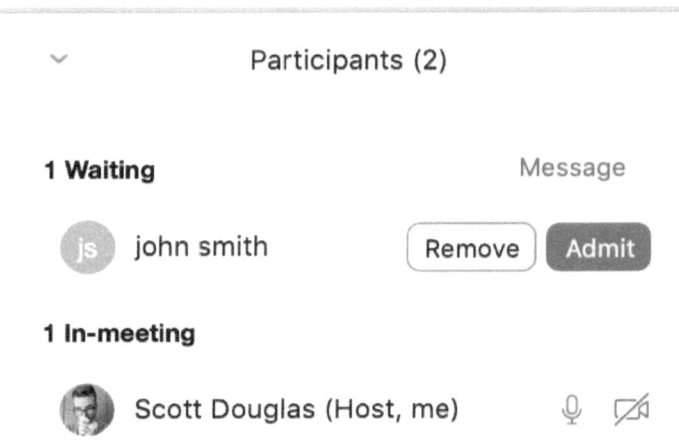

MICROPHONE SETTINGS

Most people will not want to change the microphone settings; it should update automatically based on your computer settings.

If it fails to do so, however, you can manually set both the microphone and speaker settings. To do so, click the up arrow next to the microphone icon when you are inside a conference room.

This will bring up a menu that shows all the available devices that you can connect to.

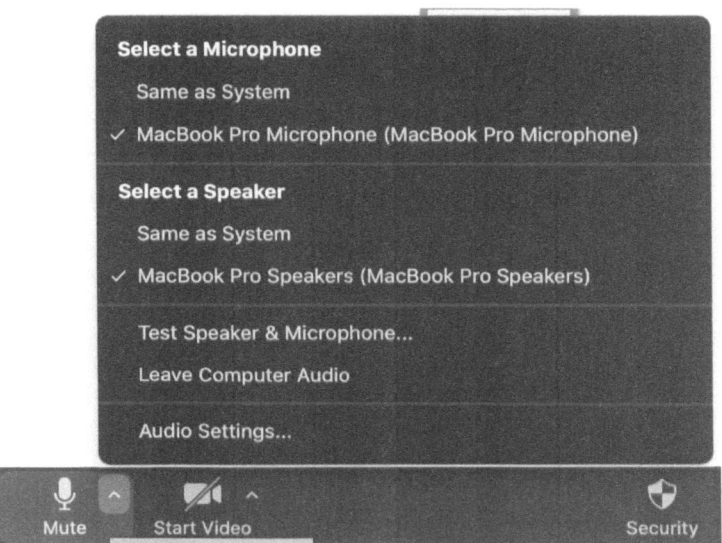

At the bottom of your screen are the main Zoom options. The first two are Mute and Start Video. If there's a red line on the icon, that means the feature is turned off. In the example below, my video is turned off but my microphone is not—so people can hear me, but not see me. You can toggle them on and off by clicking them one time.

Next is Security. This lets you select what options you are giving people who join the conference. If, for example, you want people to come into the room without you admitting them, you can click Enable Waiting Room. Keep in mind, however, that if your link was public, people can log into the conference that you don't want. We'll go over these features in more detail later in the book, so don't worry about fully understanding them now.

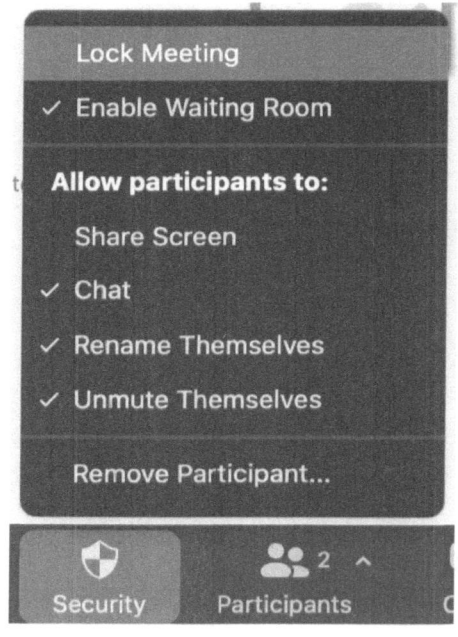

Participants opens a list of everyone in the room; Chat lets you talk to people in the room; Share Screen lets you show people what's on your computer screen—this is used if you are presenting something; and finally, Record lets you record the meeting.

To end the meeting, click the End button.

MUTING ALL

One of the most helpful features in Zoom is the Mute and Mute All. Sometimes people forget to turn their microphones off during a meeting—or there's a dog bark that's disrupting the meeting. Whatever the case, you can click on the Participants icon, then hover over the person and click the microphone next to their name; alternatively, you can go to the bottom of this screen and Mute All, to mute everyone.

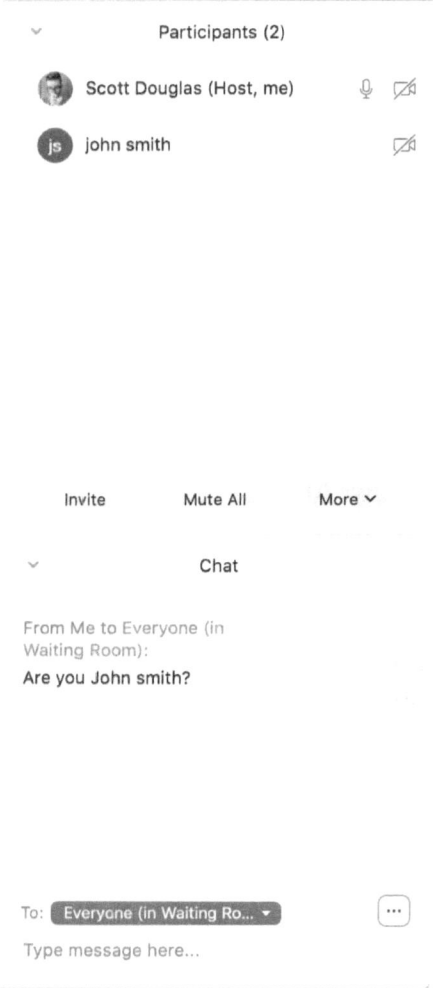

VIRTUAL BACKGROUND

The edge Zoom has over most videoconference companies is the amount they invest in more personable features. This is especially true with the popular Virtual Background feature. This lets you alter your screen to make it appear like you are somewhere besides your office.

To change your background, click the arrow next to video, then select Choose Virtual Background.

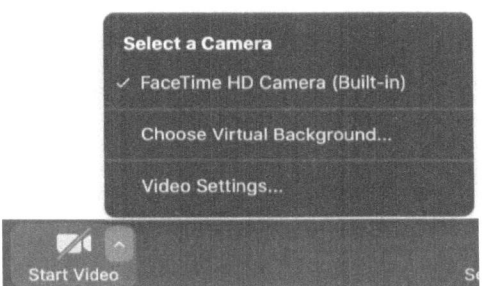

If you've never done this, you'll have to download a quick package the first time.

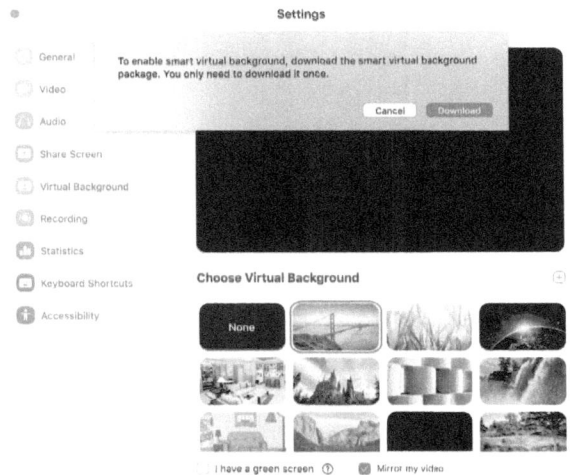

Once it's done, click the Plus button next to Choose Virtual Background. This will let you find a picture to use (hint: if you don't have one, go to google.com/image and search for Zoom backgrounds). The one I am using here is the couch from The Simpsons.

Once you have selected it, close the box. If your video is toggled on, then you'll see it immediately; if it's off, then toggle it on. This background will remain when you start the next meeting, so be careful! You may have a fun background for a more casual meeting that you want to turn off when you have a business meeting.

Rename User

Sometimes you don't want to show your full name; or maybe you're sharing Zoom with a spouse and their name is coming up instead of yours. Renaming is pretty easy in Zoom.

Click Participants on the bottom menu bar, then go to your name and click "More"; finally select Rename.

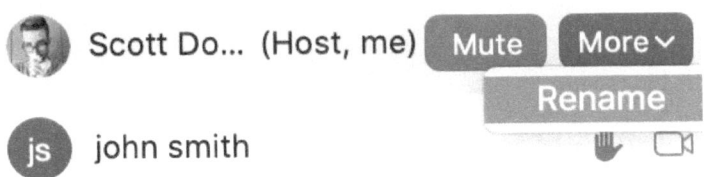

Add whatever name you want, then select the Rename button.

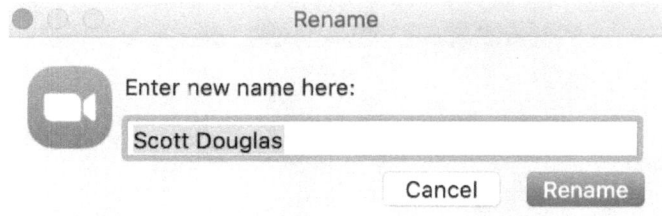

CHATTING IN ZOOM

To start a chat, click on chat in the Zoom bottom menu. By default, when you chat on Zoom, everyone in the room sees it.

If you click on Everyone, you can select one person you want to chat with. This changes the group chat to a private chat, which means only you and the other person can see it—not everyone in the conference.

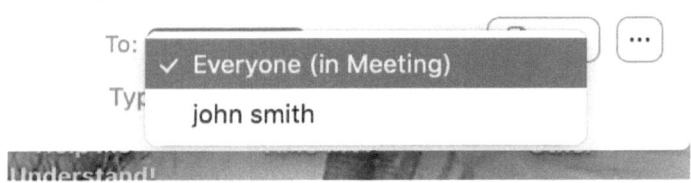

You can confirm it is a private chat by the red text that says (Privately).

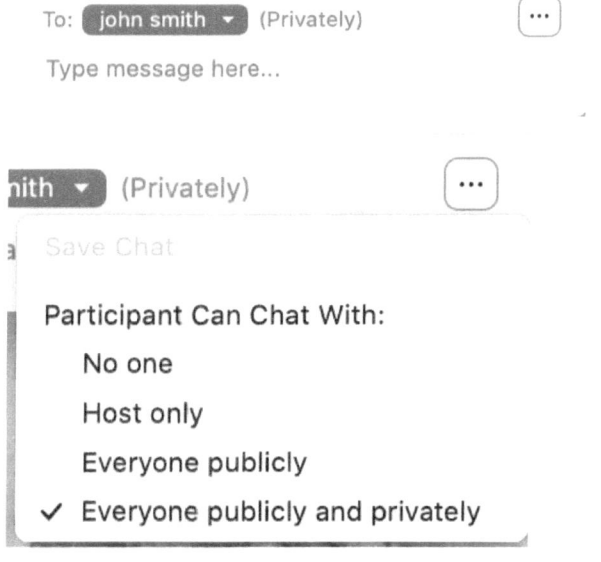

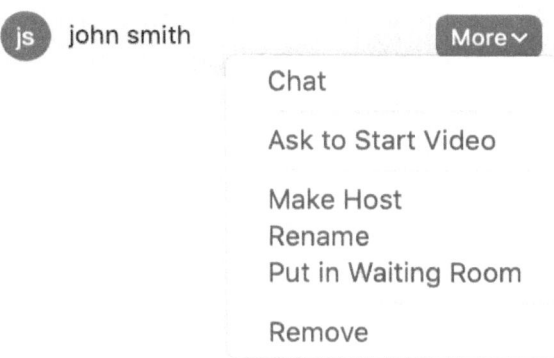

BREAKOUT SESSIONS

Breakout sessions are mini-conferences within larger conferences; as mentioned earlier, you have to turn the setting on for this to work. So if you don't see the room option, refer to the settings section and confirm that you have toggled it on.

Once you have enabled it, there are two ways to use the feature: during the conference and before the conference has started. I'll cover both ways below.

Create a Session While the Conference Is Going

When you enable Breakout Rooms, you'll see a new Breakout Rooms icon when you start your conference.

When you click the icon, you'll see options for how the room is going to be created. It can either be created automatically or manually; if it's automatic, then people are randomly assigned to the number of rooms you create. For example, if you create two rooms and ten people are in your meeting, then each room will have five people.

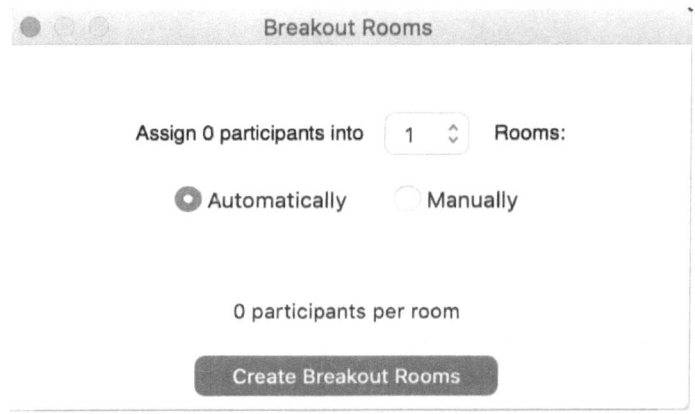

Once the rooms are created, you'll see a list of all of them. You can add a room by clicking the button at the bottom, or click Recreate to reset everything.

If you click on Options, you'll get several choices. By default, a person has to manually accept that you are putting them in a room; the first option puts them in the room automatically. You can also put a timer on the length of the breakout sessions—by default, you must manually close the rooms. And finally, the last option lets you decide how long people have to leave the rooms after you close them. It's a good idea to leave it at at least 60 seconds to give people time to finish thoughts.

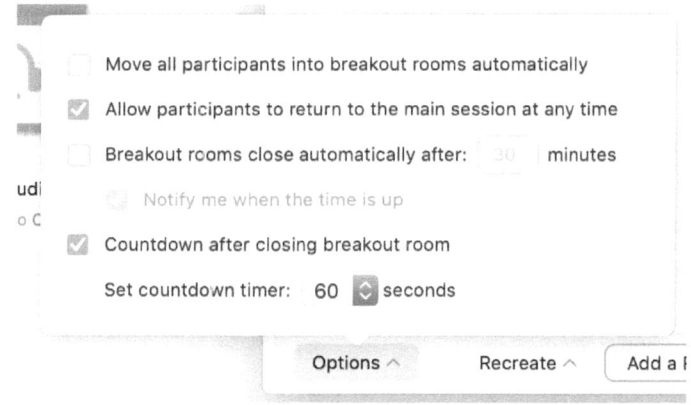

To assign someone to a room, click Assign, and then select the person's name that you are assigning.

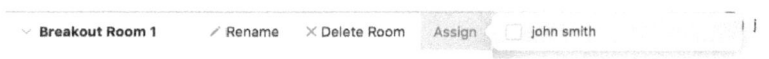

Once they are assigned, you can see all the people in each room. When you are ready to start a breakout session, click the blue Open All Rooms in the lower right corner. If you close this box, all your settings can be saved. So you can create your Breakout Rooms early in the conference, and have them ready to go for later.

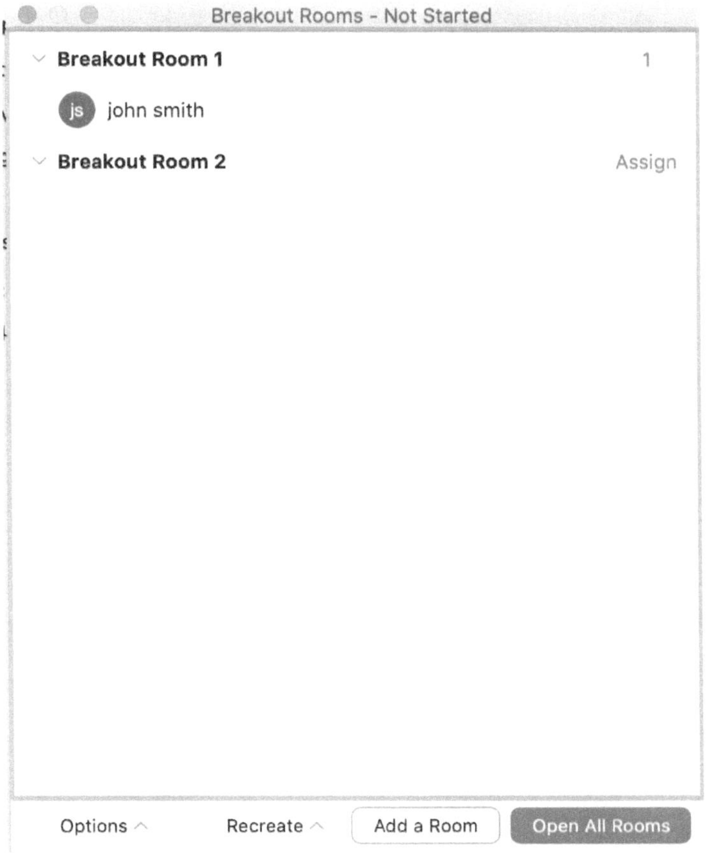

Breakout Rooms - Not Started

∨ **Breakout Room 1**	1
js john smith	
∨ **Breakout Room 2**	Assign

Options ∧   Recreate ∧   Add a Room   Open All Rooms

Once the Breakout Rooms begin, you can check the progress of who has (and has not) joined.

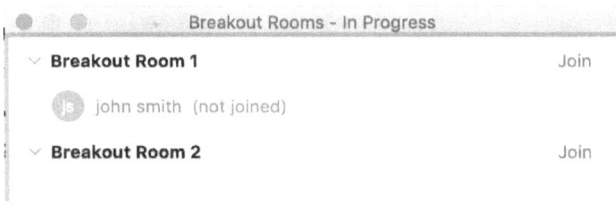

Breakout Rooms - In Progress

∨ **Breakout Room 1**   Join

    js john smith (not joined)

∨ **Breakout Room 2**   Join

As the host, you are not in a Breakout Room. You have the ability to pop into any Breakout Room that you have created to check out how things are going.

If you want to leave the Breakout Room, click End, and then select the blue Leave Breakout Room; this will return you to the main conference room.

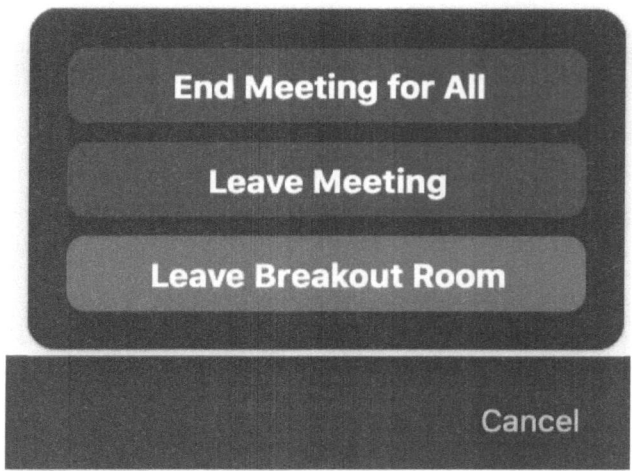

You can also broadcast a message to everyone that is inside of a Breakout Room. Click the Breakout Room icon, then select Broadcast a message to all from the lower left corner.

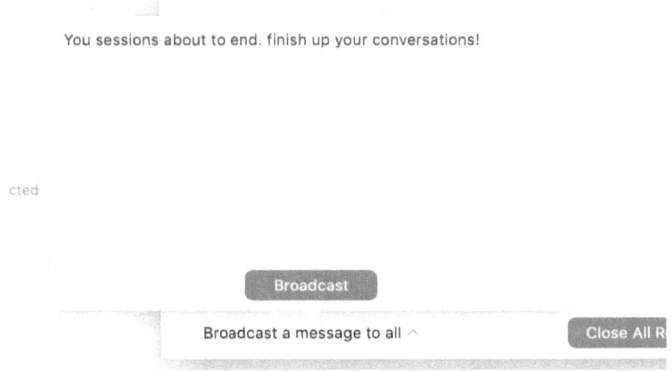

If you have not put a timer on the Breakout Rooms, then you will have to close them manually. To do this, click on the Breakout Room icon, then click the red Close All Rooms button.

You'll see a message on your interface that tells you how long users have to return to the main room. Some users will probably end early, so you will slowly start seeing them reappear in your main room.

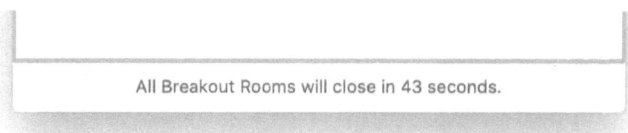

All Breakout Rooms will close in 43 seconds.

ASSIGN BREAKOUT ROOMS BEFORE THE CONFERENCE

You can also create Breakout Rooms in advance. This can be great for small businesses where everyone is using their work email. It can be problematic, however, when everyone is using non-work email; you may have one email, then the person joins the conference with another email—so when the breakout sessions start, they don't get assigned.

If you'd like to pre-assign the rooms, then schedule a meeting as you normally would. Under Meeting Options select Breakout Room pre-assign.

Meeting Options

Enable join before host

Mute participants upon entry ☑

☑ Enable waiting room

Breakout Room pre-assign

Record the meeting automatically on the local computer

When you select the option, you'll have two options: Create the rooms manually or import them from a list.

☑ **Breakout Room pre-assign**

    + Create Rooms   ⬆ Import from CSV

When you create it manually, you'll get an empty box with no one assigned.

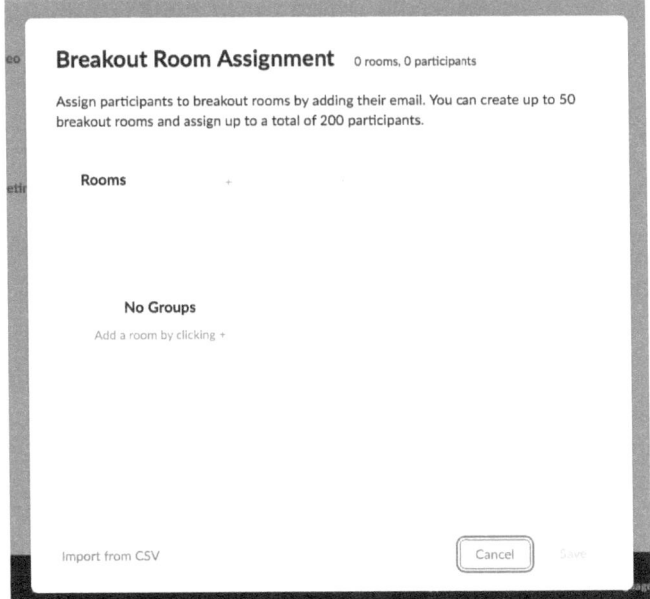

To add a room, click the + icon next to the rooms.

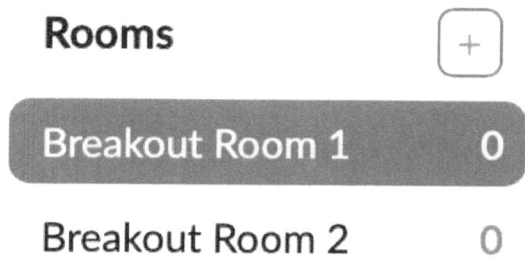

Once a room is added, you can click the pencil icon to rename it.

To add someone to the room, just add their email under Add participants and hit enter.

Breakout Room 2

> Add participants

Once you save your changes, you'll see how many rooms are assigned in your meeting notes; you can select Edit to change it.

☑ Breakout Room pre-assign

3 Breakout Rooms Edit

When you manually add people, you will need to upload a CSV file (you can export in CSV format from Excel or Numbers) using Zoom's template. When you click the import option, there is an option to download their template.

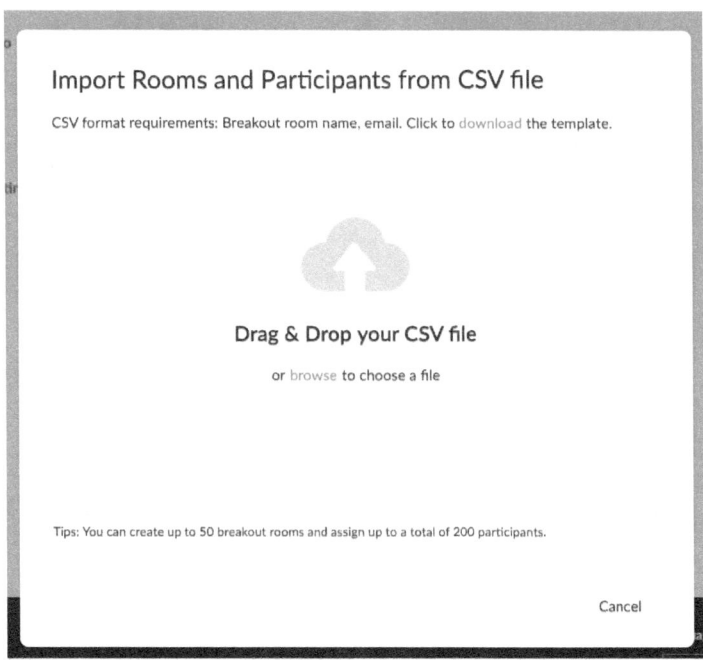

Import Rooms and Participants from CSV file

CSV format requirements: Breakout room name, email. Click to download the template.

Drag & Drop your CSV file

or browse to choose a file

Tips: You can create up to 50 breakout rooms and assign up to a total of 200 participants.

Cancel

The template is pretty straightforward; one field to name your room and one field to say who is in that room. You can add and remove rows from the template.

breakout_room_template

Pre-assign Room Name	Email Address
room1	test1@xxx.com
room1	test2@xxx.com
room2	test3@xxx.com
room2	test4@xxx.com
room3	test5@xxx.com
room3	test6@xxx.com

WINDOW VIEWS

There are several different window views for Zoom—but people have to have their video turned on to use them. So, if you're in a meeting and don't know why some of these views don't work, see if everyone is using video for the conference.

To get started go to the upper right where it says Gallery View. That's how you toggle between all the views. The open box next to Gallery View will turn your software into full-screen mode.

In full screen, you can move the thumbnail video preview boxes around your screen.

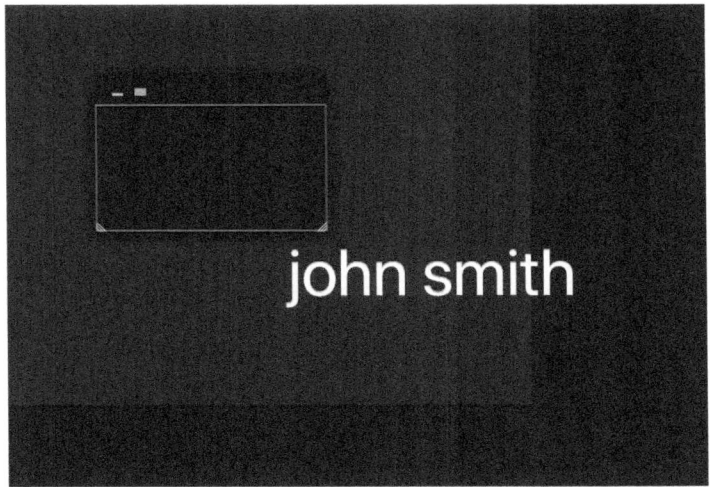

You can also minimize the boxes by clicking on the minus.

There are two views: Gallery View where you see everyone, and Speaker where you see the main speaker in a large box.

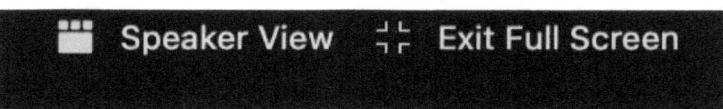

When your software is in full-screen mode on a Mac (in Gallery View), you can go to other software and have your conference windows appear as a picture-in-picture view.

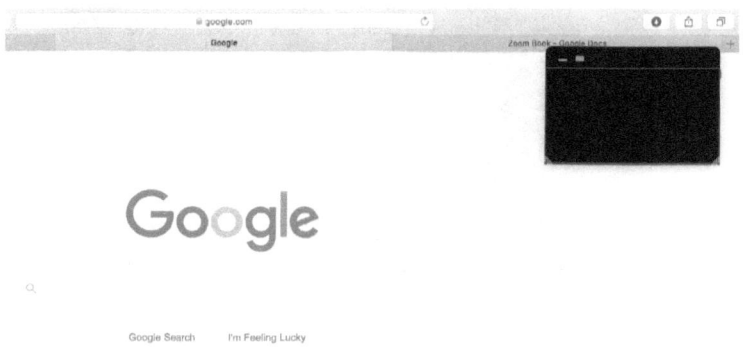

[4]

ADVANCE CONFERENCE SETTINGS

This chapter will cover:
- Conferencing settings
- Sharing your screen
- Whiteboards
- Managing people in a room

ZOOM CONFERENCE SETTINGS

There are two types of settings in Zoom. There are settings in your account; and there are settings within your conference. We covered the first settings earlier. This section will cover the second part of settings, which you can get to when your conference is open; click the drop down and select Preferences.

You'll see almost a dozen different settings that you can control. Don't worry! These are all very basic settings. And most are pretty self-explanatory.

Under General, you can select multiple monitors (if you have your laptop connected to another screen, for example); you can also change the skin tone of your reactions.

Under Video you can change the ratio and change how Gallery View is organized. You can also have it touch up your appearance...just remember, it's not a miracle worker! What this feature does is create sort of a light blur on your face to hide blemishes.

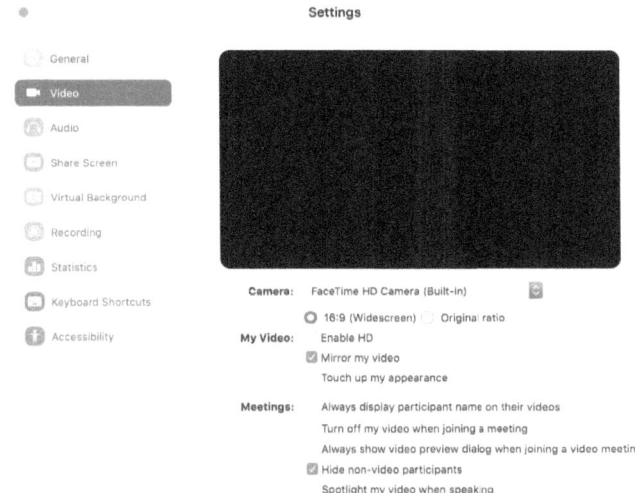

At the bottom of the Video options menu, you can get a few more options when you click the button.

If you are having trouble with your mic, you can go to the audio settings and see if it's working. When you speak, you should see the input level lighting up; if you aren't seeing that, then there's probably a problem with your mic.

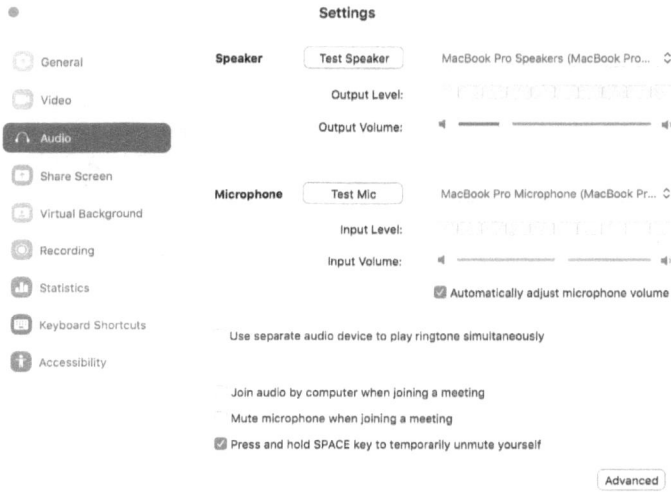

Share Screen settings updates how it looks for both you and other participants when you share your screen.

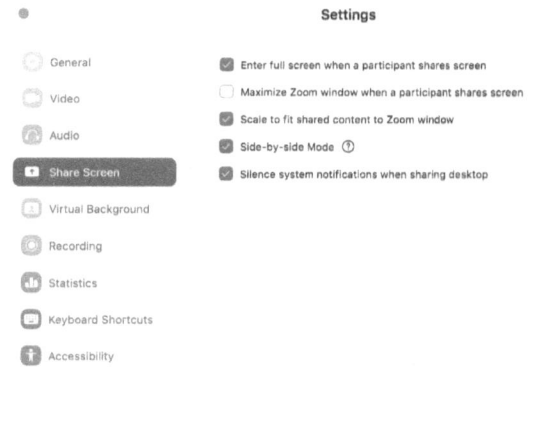

There are a few more options when you click on the Advanced button.

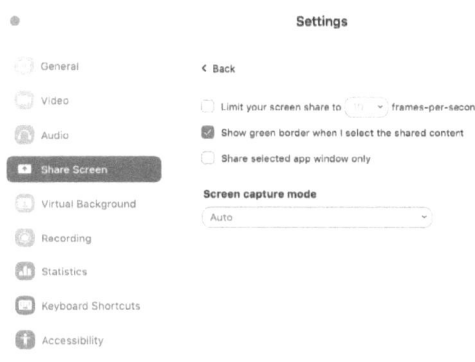

If you are recording a meeting, you can select where it's being saved in the Recording menu. You can also separate the audio of each person who speaks, which is good if you plan on editing the file later.

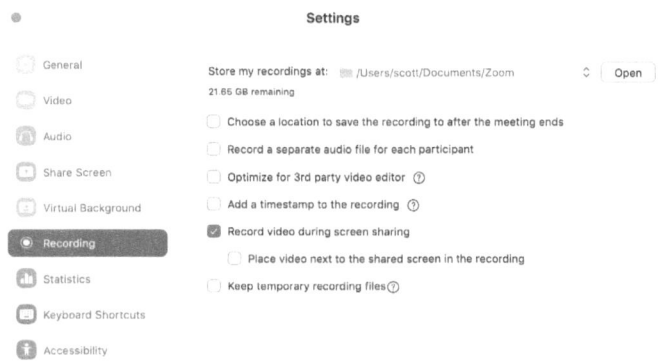

Statistics isn't very helpful unless you are having a connectivity problem; you can use this setting to see how you are connected—if you have bad bandwidth for example. It's good for troubleshooting if there's a connection problem on your end or another person's.

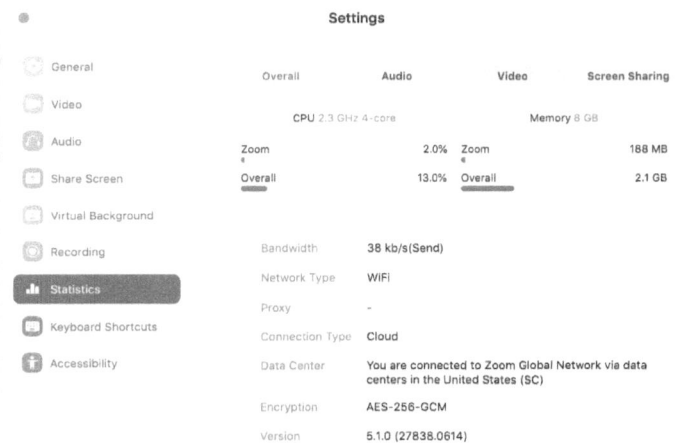

Keyboard Shortcuts lets you change the default shortcut for any function with a different key.

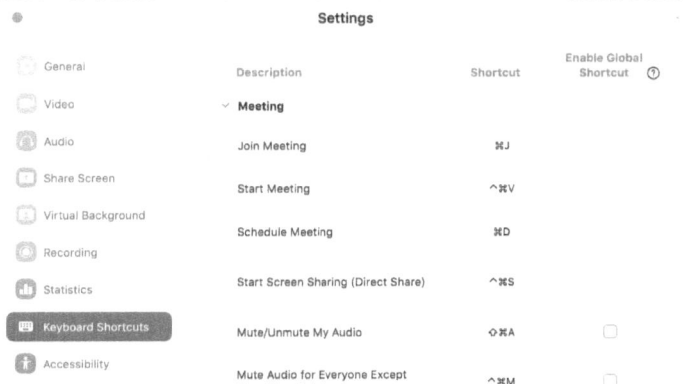

To update a shortcut, click the shortcut section and add what key command you want to use.

Accessibility is for adjusting how subtitles look—you will need to update your subtitle preference from the main setting menu as well.

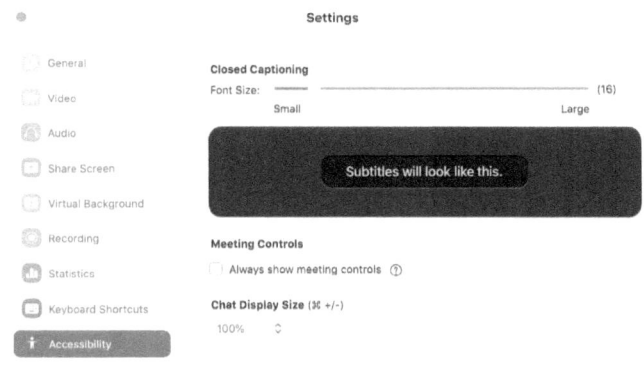

SHARING YOUR SCREEN

As the host, you can share your screen; you can also control if other people can share their screen as well.

Click the Share screen button in your bottom menu, and you can get started. The first thing it will ask is what you want to share. You can share your desktop (meaning whatever is on your computer screen), a specific window on your desktop, a

Whiteboard (covered in the next section), or a device window such as an iPhone.

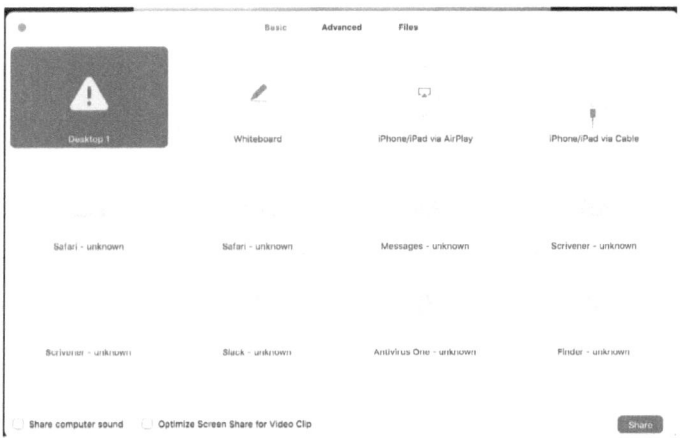

If you click the tab above, you can go to Advanced settings. From here you can select only a portion of your screen you want to share, if you only want to share sounds coming from your computer, or if you want to use a second camera.

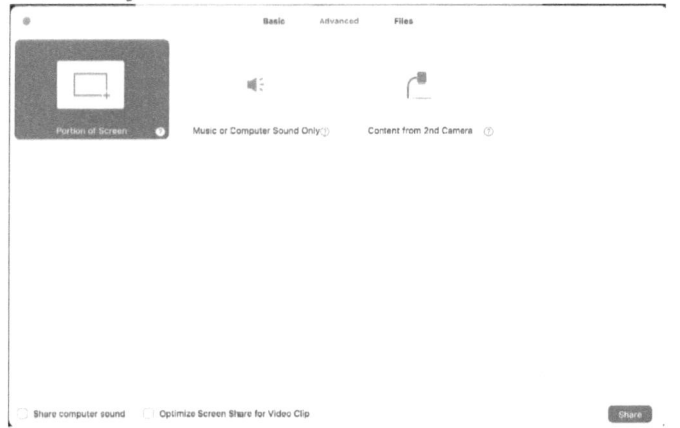

Finally, the last tab lets you share files from your computer to everyone in the meeting.

On the bottom of any of these screens, you'll see two options: one to share your computer sound (if you are sharing a screen with a video, for example, you'd want to make sure this is on); two, to optimize your screen.

☐ Share computer sound   ☐ Optimize Screen Share for Video Clip

ANNOTATIONS AND WHITEBOARDS

Under the share screen, there's also an option for a Whiteboard. A Whiteboard is a place where you can draw notes for everyone to see. It's a great way for brainstorming because others can draw on the board as well.

The functionality of the Whiteboard is very basic; you can write text on it, draw or stamp. You can also use the Spotlight button to call attention to something.

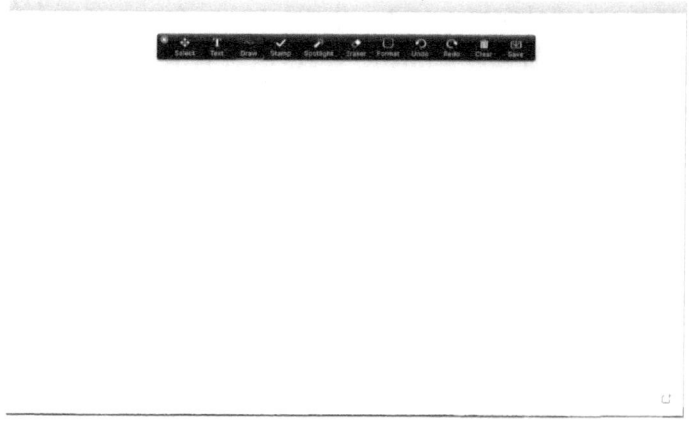

Drawing gives you several prebuilt things you can add—such as circles and squares.

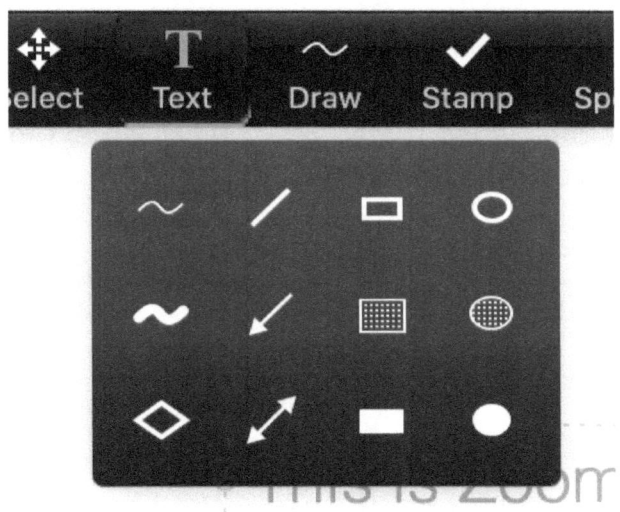

Remember, everyone sees the Whiteboard and everyone can add to it; so it can get a little messy quickly.

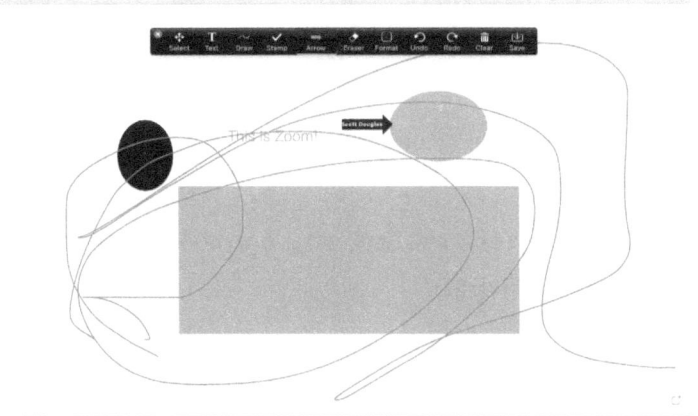

MANAGING PEOPLE IN A MEETING

As the meeting host you have the ability to manage what people can do. For example, if a person has their video turned off, you can go to More, and select Ask to Start Video.

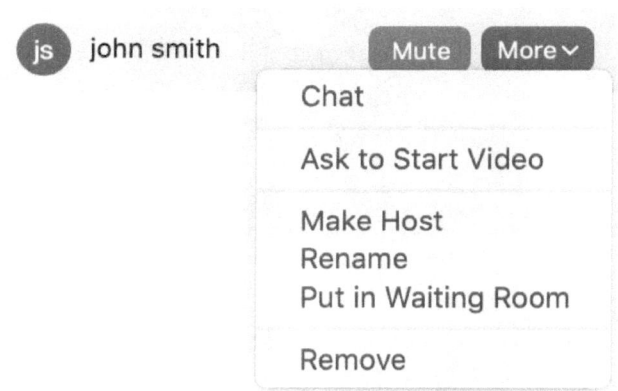

You can also mute them.

Or if they are muted, you can ask them to unmute themselves.

On the other end, the users in your meeting will be able to click a raise hand button; this is a way for them to ask a question without disrupting the meeting. You'll see a hand-raise next to their name and can acknowledge them whenever you want.

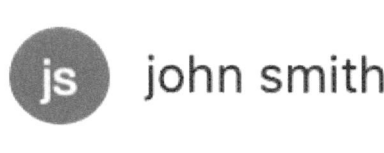

REACTIONS

When everyone has their videos turned on, they can also give reactions to the person speaking. You'll see it in your bottom toolbar tray as the last option. If you don't see it, confirm the video feed is on.

You can give two reactions: clapping and thumbs up.

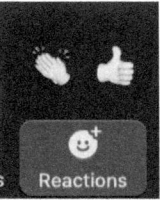

Other users will see it on their screen like the image below. Reactions can be used to keep people on mute while getting acknowledgment that they approve or understand something. When everyone has to unmute to give opinions, it can disrupt the flow of the meeting.

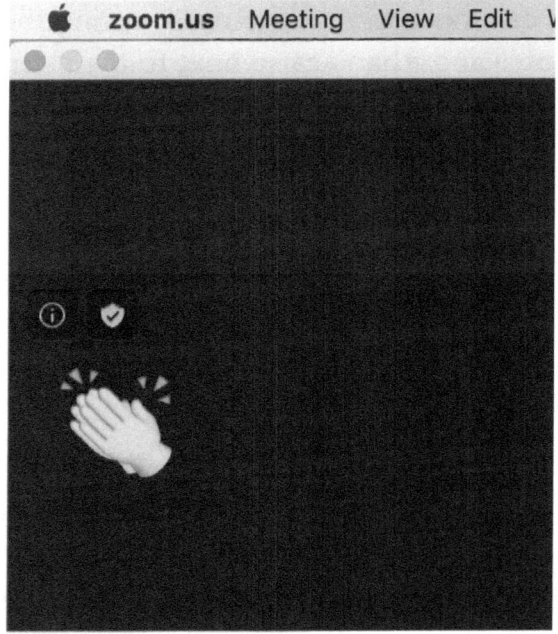

PAID FEATURES ONLY

Chances are you started Zoom on the free plan. Why not? The free plan is full of the most powerful features offered in the paid plan. So why switch? The biggest reason is probably meeting duration—nobody wants to be 39 minutes into an hour meeting only to be told your plan doesn't allow for longer than 40 minutes. All the paid plans have unlimited meeting durations.

There are other benefits to the paid plan; notably, you get a custom meeting ID, cloud recording (so no more taking up hard drive space storing meetings locally), and daily reports on how employees are using (or not using) it.

If you get to a place where you want to pay for Zoom, there are two things you want to pay attention to on the bill screen. One, if you pay yearly (all months up front) then you get a discount. And two, you need to pay for each host. What does that mean? It means if you have one host, you can only have one meeting happening at a time. If you need multiple meetings, then select the number of hosts you need.

You'll also see a number of paid add-ons—if, for example, you plan on doing webinars.

[5]
MANAGING ZOOM

This chapter will cover:
- User management
- Group management
- Room management
- Account management
- Webinars

USER MANAGEMENT

Once you pay for a subscription, several areas on the left side that have been closed will now be open. The first option is User Management.

Under User Management you can add people to your account. Just click the +Add Users button (blue) or do an import if you have a long list of users. You can also come here to search for users.

When you add a user, you can give them either a Basic or Licensed plan and also add a description of who they are.

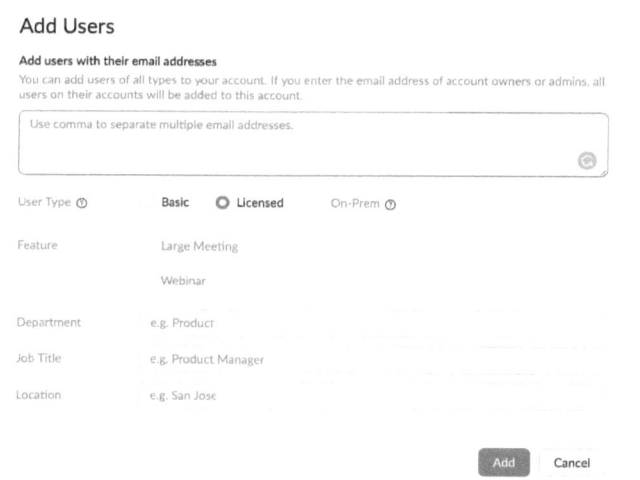

Once you add them, they'll get an email from you asking to confirm they want to be added. You'll see their name in Pending until they accept the invitation.

Finally, under Advanced, you can change the User Type for all members.

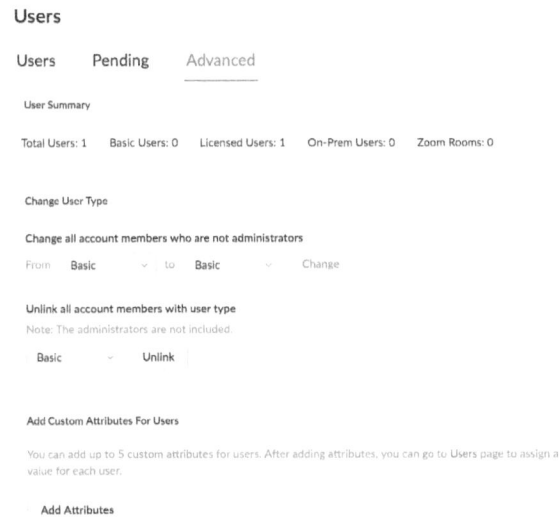

GROUP MANAGEMENT

Group Management helps you organize all your members; so, for example, you can have your IT people in one group, and Admin people in another. Then when you schedule a meeting, you can add that entire group instead of finding each person one by one. Click the blue +Add Group to get started.

This will ask you to name the group and give it a description.

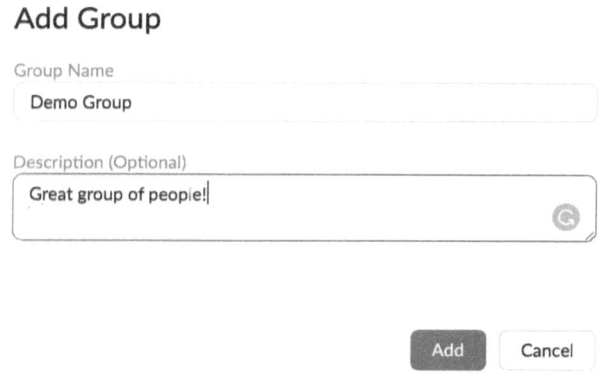

Once you click Add, you will see your group, and can click the +Add Members button in the lower right corner to start putting people in the group.

Just type their email, then click Add.

Add Members

Add Members to the group - Demo Group

Enter group member emails

Select a member

Add   Cancel

ROLE MANAGEMENT

Under Role Management, you can give admin roles to different people in your organization. Click the blue +Add Role button to get started.

Next, add their role, then click Add.

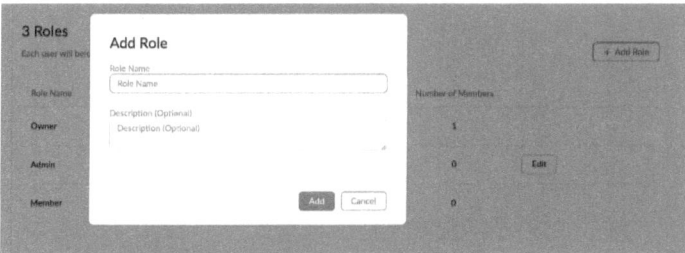

ROOM MANAGEMENT

When you have a paid account, you are also able to create private rooms with unique lock codes; to add one, go to Zoom Rooms, and select the blue +Add Room button.

Next, add your unique security code.

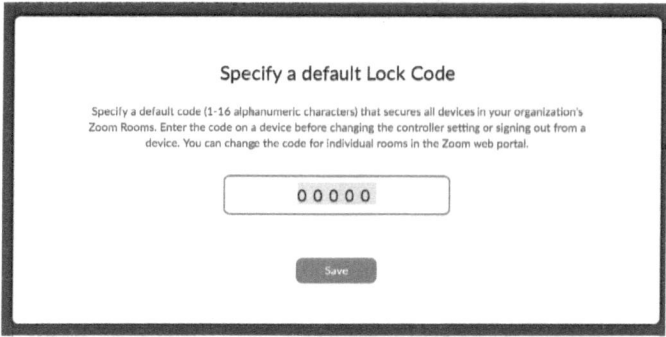

CALENDAR INTEGRATION AND DIGITAL SIGNAGE

Within Room Management there are two final options: Calendar Integration and Digital Signage Content.

Calendar Integration is pretty easy to understand—just plug in Google Calendar or whatever calendar system you use.

Digital Signage Content might be new to you. When you think of Zoom, you typically think about having a video conference; Zoom Rooms go beyond that. Digital Signage lets you use your computer like a billboard. Think about going to a fast food restaurant—those digital menus are really just digital signs.

You could technically hook up a large computer to it, but you can also buy very thin HDMI sticks for less than $200. A quick search for "Mini PC Stick" found the one below for $149. It's literally a computer that's only a few inches—small enough to fit in your pocket! You could stick one of these into your HDTV and no one would be able to see it.

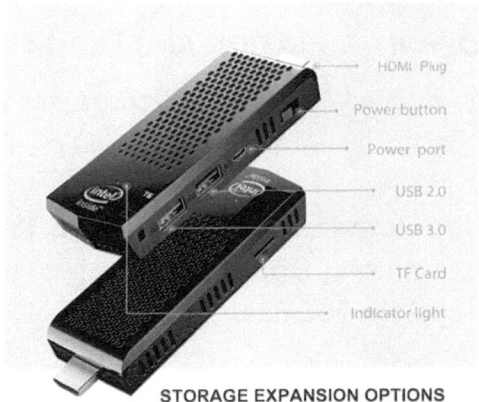

STORAGE EXPANSION OPTIONS

To add digital signage just click on the option to manage your displays.

When you add a room under Zoom Room, there's a drop-down option for digital signage display.

Add a Zoom Room

Room Name

This field is required.

+ Add a Calendar

You can add a calendar service for easy arrangement for your Zoom Rooms' meetings.

Room Type

Digital Signage Only

Zoom Room

Scheduling Display Only

Digital Signage Only

Once you have the room added, add your location. Once the room is added, you'll get an email with the activation code. Open the computer you are going to show the signage on, open up Zoom, and add the code. It's pretty simple—much more simple and cheaper than many of the digital signage companies out there!

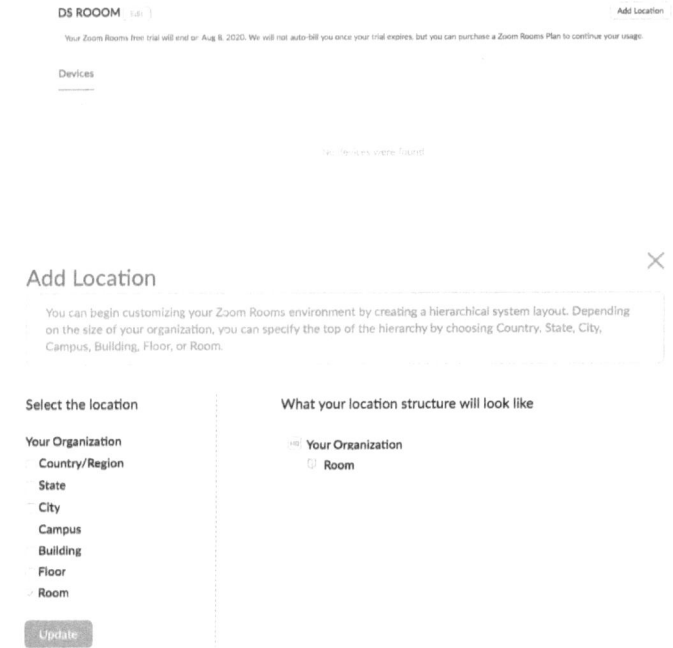

Once your location is added, you can go to digital signage and start adding your content. There are companies that will create content for a fee, but many people just create it in PowerPoint or Keynote using a template, then export it as a JPEG.

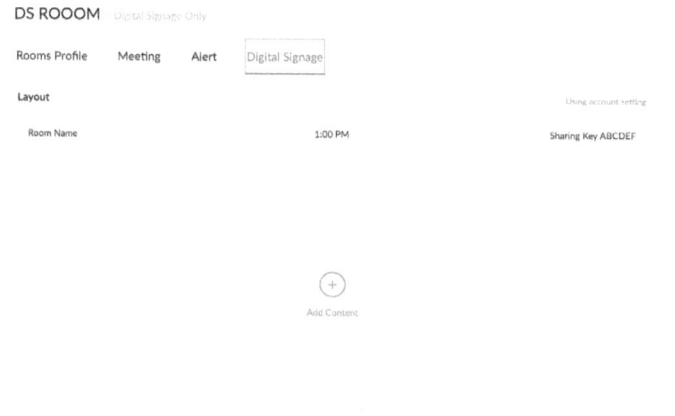

When you add content, you can create a playlist of sorts; so you can schedule exactly when the content will play. You could have it showing a lunch menu until 3:00, then switch automatically to a dinner menu at a set time.

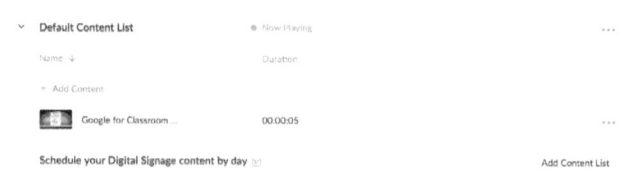

ACCOUNT MANAGEMENT

Account Management is important for one important reason: It's where you can cancel, edit, or upgrade your plan. Once you have an active plan, you can click the Cancel or Edit button at any time to remove or update the subscription.

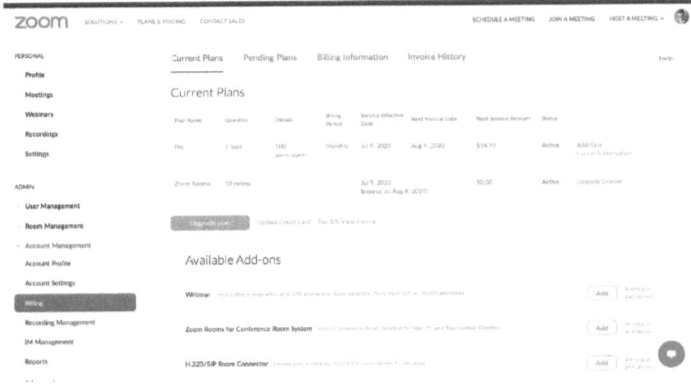

Below this screen is also were you can add various add-ons (such as webinars).

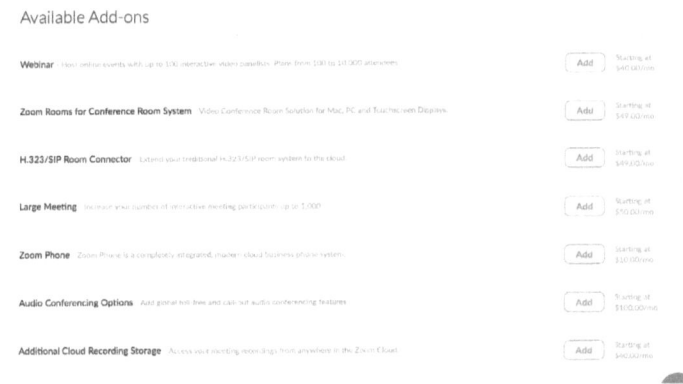

Under Account Management you can also get reports on Zoom usage by user.

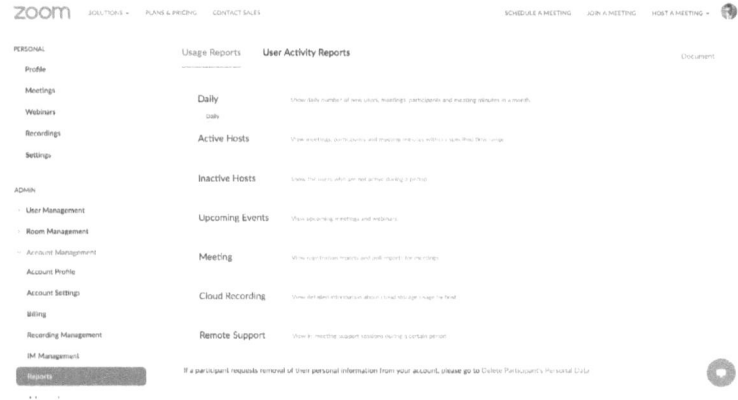

And add instant messaging groups.

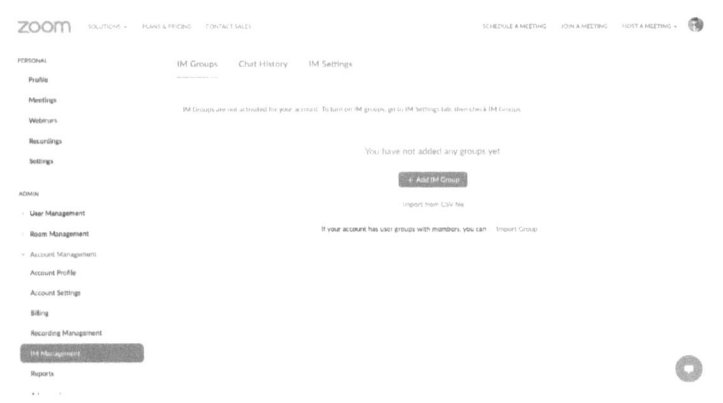

ADVANCED

Advanced has a lot of features most people will not use. You can add Branding, for example (but at a premium price) and extra security (again, at a premium).

⌄ Advanced

App Marketplace

H.323/SIP Room Connector

Meeting Connector

Branding

Security

Single Sign-On

Integration

What you will find under Advanced that you might use is Apps. Just like your phone has apps, so does Zoom; these are mini add-ons (many are free) that enhance Zoom. Adding the Slack add-on, for example, let's you open up conferences within your Slack channel.

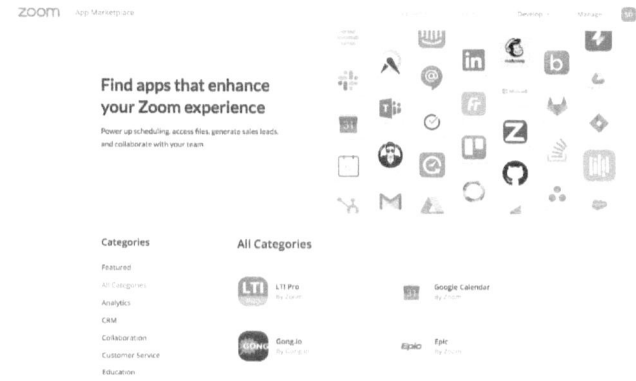

WEBINARS

Webinars probably won't be for most users. At $50 a month, it's only something you want to add when you are read to actually host Webinars.

The advantage of hosting a Webinar here versus other places is you can charge money for people to attend it. There are also most extra features you don't see on some platforms—like taking polls and adding your own branding.

ABOUT THE AUTHOR

Scott La Counte is a librarian and writer. His first book, Quiet, *Please: Dispatches from a Public Librarian* (Da Capo 2008) was the editor's choice for the Chicago Tribune and a Discovery title for the Los Angeles Times; in 2011, he published the YA book The N00b Warriors, which became a #1 Amazon bestseller; his most recent book is *#OrganicJesus: Finding Your Way to an Unprocessed, GMO-Free Christianity* (Kregel 2016). His most recent non-technical book is *Jesus Ascended. What Does That Mean?*

He has written dozens of best-selling how-to guides on tech products.

You can connect with him at ScottDouglas.org.

www.ingramcontent.com/pod-product-compliance
Lightning Source LLC
Chambersburg PA
CBHW020552220526
45463CB00006B/2268